A NOTE TO PARENTS

When your children are ready to "step into reading," giving them the right books—and lots of them—is as crucial as giving them the right food to eat. **Step into Reading Books** present exciting stories and information reinforced with lively, colorful illustrations that make learning to read fun, satisfying, and worthwhile. They are priced so that acquiring an entire library of them is affordable. And they are beginning readers with an important difference—they're written on four levels.

Step 1 Books, with their very large type and extremely simple vocabulary, have been created for the very youngest readers. **Step 2 Books** are both longer and slightly more difficult. **Step 3 Books,** written to mid-second-grade reading levels, are for the child who has acquired even greater reading skills. **Step 4 Books** offer exciting nonfiction for the increasingly proficient reader.

W9-CML-477

To Madeleine
—G. S.

The author would like to thank the persons
who spoke to him about the incidents
in this book.

Text copyright © 1992 by George Shea. Illustrations copyright © 1992 by Marshall H. Peck III.
All rights reserved under International and Pan-American Copyright Conventions. Published in the
United States by Random House, Inc., New York, and simultaneously in Canada by Random House
of Canada Limited, Toronto.

Library of Congress Cataloging-in-Publication Data
Shea, George.
    Amazing rescues / by George Shea ; illustrated by Marshall H. Peck III.
      p.   cm. – (Step into reading. A Step 3 book)
    Summary: Describes remarkable rescues in such situations as a skydiving accident, an
    alligator attack, and a fall down a well.
    ISBN 0-679-81107-9 (pbk.) – ISBN 0-679-91107-3 (lib. bdg.)
    1. Rescue work–Juvenile literature.   [1. Rescue work.]
I.   Title.   II. Series: Step into reading. Step 3 book.
  TH9402.S54   1992   628.9–dc20   90-53221

Manufactured in the United States of America   10 9 8 7 6 5 4 3 2 1

STEP INTO READING is a trademark of Random House, Inc.

AMAZING RESCUES

By George Shea

Illustrated by Marshall H. Peck III

A Step 3 Book

Random House 🏠 New York

Amazing Rescue
in the Air

Arizona, 1987.

A big group of skydivers is boarding an old DC-4 airplane. Everyone is excited. Today the divers will jump in teams, and there are some thrilling dives planned.

Each team will free-fall together. Some will form circles; some, snowflakes and other patterns. At the last moment, the divers will open their parachutes and float safely to the ground.

But skydiving is a dangerous sport. Accidents can happen.

The plane takes off. At 13,500 feet, the hatch is opened, and divers start jumping out.

A diver named Gregory stands near the hatch. It is his job to see that everyone jumps safely. He will jump last.

Gregory has made more than 1,500 jumps. He is one of the best skydivers in the United States.

It's the last team's turn. The six divers are going to make a circle in the air.

Four of the divers hold hands and jump out of the plane together. The other two–Alex and Debbie–jump next. Alex goes down to join the group.

So far, everything is going as planned.

But suddenly things start to go wrong.

A blast of air blows one diver—Guy—right out of the circle.

At the same moment, Alex joins the three divers who are still together. But Alex is falling too fast. He makes the group fall faster.

Now it is Debbie's turn to join the circle. And Guy has to get back too.

They both tuck their heads in for a fast fall.

But there is a big problem. Debbie can't see Guy. And Guy can't see Debbie. And they are zooming toward each other!

Gregory—the last to dive—sees the whole thing.

Alex

Guy

Debbie

Gregory

A second later, it happens.

Debbie smashes into Guy's backpack. Then her body snaps around. Again she bangs into Guy very hard.

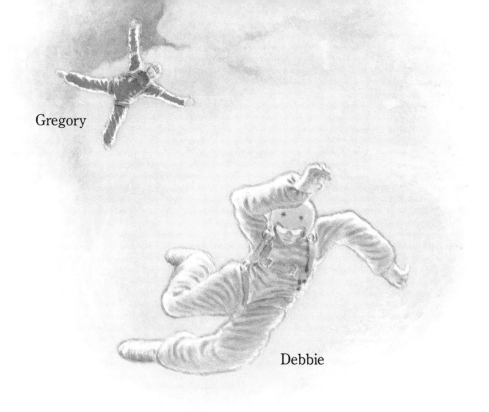

Gregory

Debbie

Gregory can tell that Guy is still conscious. Even though he is hurt, Guy will be able to open his chute and land safely.

But Debbie looks like a rag doll spinning in space. Gregory can see she is unconscious. Her chute won't open unless she pulls the rip cord. And she won't come to in time.

Instantly, Gregory goes into a fast dive. Head tucked. Arms at his sides. Legs together. Toes pointed.

He looks like Superman, diving through the sky. In fifteen seconds he drops more than 3,000 feet.

He has only twelve seconds left before he and Debbie hit the ground.

When Gregory catches up with
Debbie, he grabs her strap to stop her
spinning. With his other hand he pulls her
rip cord, and then lets go.

Debbie's chute opens.

But the ground is rushing up.
Gregory pulls his own rip cord.

Gregory's chute opens. Seconds later,
he lands.

The rescue has taken only twenty-five
seconds!

Debbie hits the ground, still unconscious. But she is alive!

A helicopter takes her to a hospital. She has many injuries, including nine broken ribs. But she is going to be all right.

People call Gregory "Superman," but he is a real-life hero without superhuman powers. He saw what had to be done to save somebody's life. And he did it!

Amazing Rescue
in the Water

Florida, 1951.

A girl and boy are fishing at a small lake. They laugh as they scoop little fish out of the water and drop them into their bucket.

But there is something besides little fish lurking in the water. An eight-foot-long alligator! It is watching them.

And waiting.

The bucket is full. The boy goes up the hill to get another bucket.

The girl is alone.

The alligator sees its chance. It swims in closer.

Suddenly, it leaps high out of the water and sinks its big sharp teeth into the girl's arm!

The girl screams and fights to free herself. But the alligator's grip is too tight. She can't get loose.

The huge reptile drags the girl into the water. Then it twists and turns wildly, trying to break her bones.

The boy hears her screams and runs down the hill and into the water. He grabs the girl and tries to pull her away from the alligator. But the alligator is not about to let go.

The boy tries everything he can think of. He yells. He waves his arms. He waves his shirt. He hits the alligator with a stick.

But he can't get the alligator to pay attention to him.

Finally, the boy wraps his legs around some roots on the bank. He hangs out over the water as far as he can. He waves his arms.

The alligator looks up at the boy. For just one moment it forgets the girl.

Its jaws open.

Instantly, the boy grabs the girl and yanks her free.

He drags her up onto the shore. The alligator starts after them.

The boy pushes the girl up the hill. She is still alive, but she is too weak to walk.

The girl is bleeding badly. If she doesn't get medical help, she will die.

The boy puts the girl on the handlebars of his bike. Then he pedals down the road as fast as he can.

Finally, he sees a building—a garage.
One of the workers there drives the girl to
the hospital. The girl's arm is badly cut
and broken, but she is going to be okay.

The next day wildlife officers lasso the alligator. They take it to a swamp in the Everglades, where thousands of alligators live. It can't hurt people there.

The boy is a hero. He receives a medal for bravery from the President of the United States.

Amazing Rescue
Underground

Texas, 1987.

Some little children are playing in the backyard. In this yard there is a very deep hole—an old abandoned water well. It is covered by a rock. The opening is only eight inches wide.

It doesn't look very big. But it's big enough for a very small child to fall through!

Suddenly, a telephone rings inside the house. Jessica's mother goes to answer it. A few minutes later, she comes back outside.

Jessica has disappeared.

The other children are standing by the hole. The rock isn't covering it anymore.

Jessica has fallen in!

Jessica's mother calls her name.

There is no answer. She runs back into the house and dials 911.

Deep down inside the hole, little
Jessica can hear someone calling to her.
But she can't move.
She is stuck halfway down the well.
Twenty-two feet below the ground!

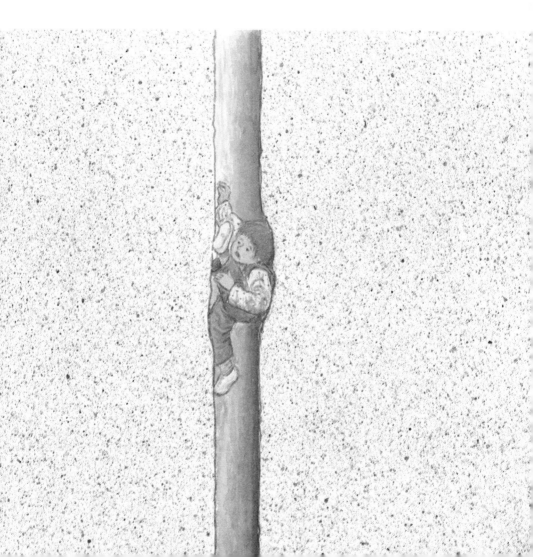

Three minutes later, help arrives: a police car, an ambulance, and a fire engine.

A rescue worker shines his flashlight into the hole. He can't see Jessica. He calls her name.

"Jessica! Jessica!"

Finally, he hears a sound. A tiny little cry coming from far below.

Rescue workers lower a hose into the hole. They pump air down so Jessica can breathe.

Then they lower a tiny microphone. They can hear Jessica crying.

The backyard is filling up with people. Some come to work. Some come to watch.

Jessica's father arrives in a police car. He and Jessica's mother have to sit and wait. Is their baby going to be okay?

The rescue workers tear down the fence. A big digging machine rumbles into the yard. It is called a backhoe.

The backhoe starts to dig a hole beside the one where Jessica is trapped.

It digs down two feet and stops. Solid rock!

They are going to need something more powerful than a backhoe.

A new digging machine comes into the yard. It is called a rathole rig. It can cut through rock.

But the work is slow.

How long can Jessica hold out?

Now it is nighttime. The rathole rig is still drilling.

Many people come from all over to help. Newspaper and TV reporters are on the scene. Jessica has been in the hole for ten hours!

The night air is cold. Too cold for a little girl in play clothes who can't move. Special heating tanks are brought into the yard. They start pumping warm air down to Jessica.

Jessica's mother sings to her. And she sings back:

"Winnie the Pooh, Winnie the Pooh, chubby little cubby, all stuffed with fluff..."

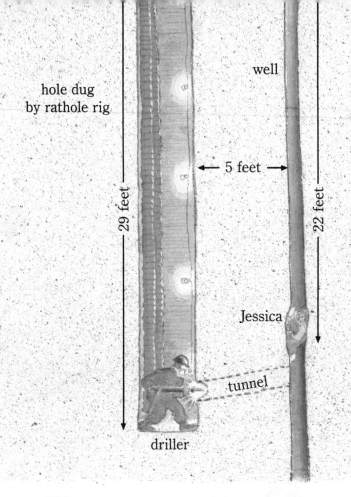

hole dug
by rathole rig

well

← 5 feet →

29 feet

22 feet

Jessica

tunnel

driller

The next step will be to drill a tunnel five feet long–across to the well. The tunnel will break through just below where Jessica is stuck.

That way, rock will not fall on Jessica.

Every minute counts. What if Jessica slips down farther? What if she dies before they reach her?

The rathole rig will not fit in the hole. Now the job is much harder. The rescue workers will have to dig the tunnel with hand-drills.

A man is lowered into the hole. He's twenty-nine feet under the ground. He begins to drill through the rock.

The tunnel is getting longer. Now the driller must lie on his stomach. It is a tight squeeze.

The drill is heavy. The man is strong, but the work is hard. After a half hour another man must take his place.

The men can drill only two inches an hour. But they are getting closer. And each man is able to wiggle just a little farther into the tunnel.

They can hear Jessica crying. That keeps them going. She has been in the hole for two days!

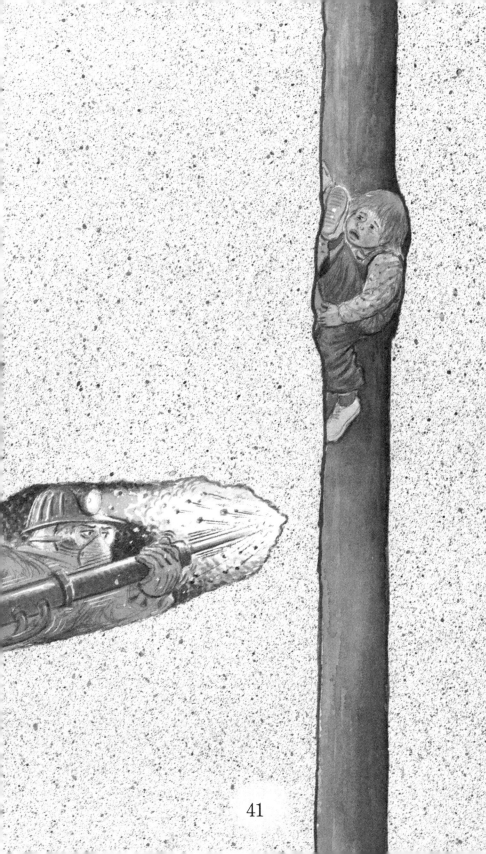

They are very close. They have broken through into the well. Now they must be extra careful.

The driller uses a special drill. It cuts rock with a powerful spray of water. The spray does not come near Jessica.

Two paramedics go down. One spreads petroleum jelly all over the walls of the tunnel. It will help Jessica slide.

He takes hold of Jessica's leg and begins to pull. The pulling hurts her, but he keeps pulling, very slowly. Inch by inch, she starts to slide along the tunnel.

Suddenly, he is holding her. Jessica isn't crying. She is calm and quiet.

The second man wraps her in pads, ties her to a board, and holds her close.

A cable pulls them up.

Up above, everyone is waiting.

The paramedic's head comes out of the hole. He is holding Jessica. But she is not moving.

No one speaks, no one moves.

Then the crowd sees Jessica's eyes. They are wide open. Everyone starts to cheer and cry at the same time. The millions of people who are watching on TV cry too.

Jessica is alive!

An ambulance takes Jessica to the
hospital. She has some injuries, but she is
going to be all right.

Jessica is a very brave little girl. She is only one and a half years old.

A very young survivor!